HUMAN DEVELOPMENT

NICHOLAS TUCKER

ADOLESCENCE

HUMAN DEVELOPMENT
ADOLESCENCE

Adolescence

Adulthood

Childhood

Old Age

Series editor: Marcella Streets
Series design: Helen White
Series consultant: Dr John Coleman

First published in 1990
by Wayland (Publishers) Ltd
61 Western Road, Hove
East Sussex, BN3 1JD, England

British Library Cataloguing in Publication Data
Tucker, Nicholas
  Adolescence. – (Human development).
  1. Adolescence
  I. Title II. Series
  305.235

  ISBN 1 85210 913 0

Phototypeset by N. Taylor & R. Gibbs, Wayland
Printed in Italy by Rotolito Lombarda S.p.A.
Bound in France by A.G.M.

CONTENTS

INTRODUCTION 4

PHYSICAL DEVELOPMENT 8

SEXUAL DEVELOPMENT 16

MENTAL GROWTH 24

FAMILY RELATIONSHIPS 32

FRIENDS, SCHOOL AND LEISURE 41

IDENTITY 46

PROBLEMS DURING ADOLESCENCE 52

GLOSSARY 62

BOOKS AND VIDEOS 63

INDEX 64

iNTRODuCTiON

ADOLESCENCE IS the period of life between childhood and adulthood. It begins with puberty, a time of rapid growth and sexual development.

Few adolescents are as glamorous and self-confident as this image suggests. Most need help and encouragement as they adjust to physical and emotional changes.

While all human beings go through the physical changes of puberty, not all societies recognize the period known as adolescence as a distinct phase of development. In some East African societies, for example, children go through a ceremony to mark their passage into adulthood. The advantage of this is that it avoids the confusion many societies have over when an adolescent should be accorded adult privileges and responsibilities. This confusion is particularly evident in the Western world. For example, in Britain you can marry at sixteen with parental consent but are not allowed to drive until seventeen; you cannot vote, watch certain films or buy alcohol until eighteen years of age.

In pre-industrial Western societies children usually started adult labour at a very early age. Working with adults, they dressed like them and would often behave like them too. After a long day's work, they had little time or energy left over to be with friends.

In the developed world, today's adolescents have to wait a long time before they are considered adults, are allowed to work at adult jobs and are accorded adult rights and privileges. In fact adolescence now lasts for a much longer time than it did in the past. This is partly because young people spend so many more years at school now. Although an adolescent may be physically and mentally mature, they may still be financially dependent on their parents. They may still be treated like children at home and at school.

This confusion of status can lead many adolescents to resent the way they are sometimes treated and to complain about it. Adults may also feel resentment towards adolescents. Young people can make adults uncomfortably aware that they are growing old; adults may occasionally feel jealous of the strength and energy of the young.

Adolescents can also sometimes seem very threatening to adults. This is partly because adolescence is often depicted as a problem time, particularly by the media. Problems do arise in some families, because it is a period of change. Parents have to get used to the idea that their children are growing up, and adolescents are trying out different types of behaviour, learning to cope with their changing bodies and adjusting to their new roles in society. However, most adolescents manage to get through this period unscathed. In fact, sometimes they grow closer to their parents, especially if they find they have more interests in common. The increase in physical and mental skills during adolescence, together with more freedom, can make it a really exciting time of life.

Adolescents are subject to many different influences. While they inherit many characteristics from their parents, they are also very much affected by other factors, such as living conditions, schooling and upbringing.

In this book we will be looking at how human beings develop during adolescence. First of all we will look at the physical changes that occur during puberty and how these affect adolescents' feelings about themselves. Moving on to mental growth, we will discuss typical changes in adolescent thought patterns and how these developments are encouraged

Child or adult? In many societies, the status of adolescents like this young mother is not clearly defined.

in school. We will then look at the role that family relationships and friendship play in adolescent life.

Adolescents often become very involved in working out exactly how they see themselves. We will look at how they begin to stand back and look at themselves from the point of view of others in an attempt to discover their true identity – their 'real' self. The final chapter deals with some of the problems that, although not exclusive to adolescence, tend to arise for some people during this period of development.

PHYSICAL DEVELOPMENT

THIS CHAPTER concentrates on puberty, the name given to the changes to the body that occur during adolescence.

Adolescents sometimes feel self-conscious about their height or weight.

HOW PUBERTY STARTS

Puberty is caused by a shift in the level of hormones produced by the brain. Hormones are chemical substances and are present in the body from birth. Puberty takes place when part of the brain known as the hypothalamus has developed sufficiently to send large numbers of hormones to the pituitary gland. This gland is also in the brain. The pituitary gland is triggered into releasing increased amounts of FSH (Follicle Stimulating Hormone) and LH (Luteinizing Hormone). These hormones are responsible for ova (eggs) to start being released from girls' ovaries, and sperm being produced in boys' testes. The ovaries and testes then produce sex hormones, including testosterone in boys and oestrogen in girls. These sex hormones trigger other changes in the body, such as breast development and the growth of body hair.

HEIGHT

The first obvious indication that puberty is beginning is usually a rapid increase in height. This 'growth spurt' usually starts at around ten years old for girls and twelve years old for boys, though there are wide individual variations. Undernourishment, for example, can delay puberty. During the growth spurt, boys and girls may grow up to ten centimetres each year. In early puberty girls tend to be taller than boys, but by fourteen years old most boys have caught up with – or overtaken – them. By seventeen, girls have usually reached their adult

Body shape changes during adolescence. This boy's legs and arms seem very long but the rest of his body will soon catch up.

height, but boys sometimes continue growing until they are nineteen years old.

Those who start their growth spurt quite early may feel more confident at suddenly being taller than their friends, although some feel self-conscious and awkward.

The age at which adolescents begin their growth spurt is not necessarily an indication of how tall they will be later on. Adult height depends on general health and parental height. A good diet, involving plenty of body-building proteins, also helps promote growth. Children who have been small for their age up to this point tend to stay small through adolescence as well.

WEIGHT AND SHAPE

Both boys and girls put on weight during adolescence. To begin with, girls usually outweigh boys, but by fourteen years old boys are generally heavier. Physical shape also changes. Girls start developing breasts and broader hips, while boys become more muscular, particularly in their shoulders. Face shape changes too, with the nose and jaw becoming more prominent. These changes do not always happen at the same time, so a nose can sometimes look too large for the face it may have temporarily outgrown; legs and arms may seem very long and lanky until the rest of the body catches up with them.

BODY HAIR

The hormones responsible for increases in height and weight also trigger the growth of hair on the face, arms, legs and in the pubic area. Later on, boys develop hair on the chest, and both sexes may grow hair on the abdomen. There may also be a little hair on hands, feet and the back. At first all body hair is soft and sparse, but it gradually grows coarser and thicker.

Some boys and girls welcome this hair growth as a sign of their increasing maturity, but others feel embarrassed by it or prefer to remove it, especially if the hair is very dark and noticeable. In some cultures it is fashionable for women in particular to remove certain areas of body hair, for example from their legs, underarm area and face.

OTHER CHANGES

In addition to these visible changes in the body, there are many invisible changes. There are changes in the internal sex organs (see the next chapter), and in the main organs of the body. For example, the heart almost doubles in weight and the lungs suddenly increase in size. Blood pressure and the number of red blood cells in the body also increase during puberty. These increases are greater in boys than girls. Both sexes experience a noticeable increase in their physical strength and endurance at this time. These changes are just as likely to make adolescents feel 'different' as the more obvious ones are.

Physical changes during adolescence.

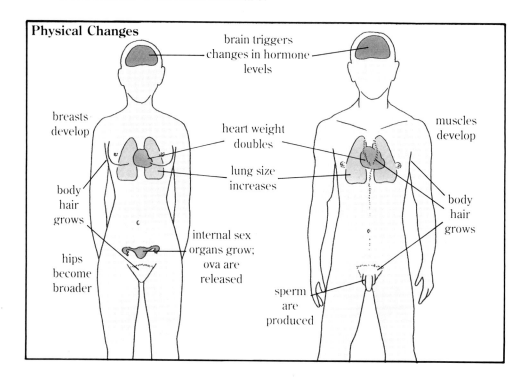

Physical Changes

brain triggers changes in hormone levels

breasts develop

heart weight doubles

lung size increases

muscles develop

body hair grows

body hair grows

hips become broader

internal sex organs grow; ova are released

sperm are produced

In some cultures, tests of physical strength are used to prove that boys have reached manhood. This Indonesian boy has to jump over a high wall.

13

Boys also experience a change in the pitch of their voices during adolescence. As the voice-box grows, the voice becomes slightly croaky and then deeper. This usually happens after the growth spurt has begun.

BODY *image*

During this time of rapid physical change, young people sometimes worry that they are not going to end up looking as they would wish. This anxiety is increased by the huge importance many societies attach to physical appearance. Children's fairy stories of beautiful princesses and handsome princes can start these worries. Later the use of glamorous young people in advertising, films and television continues this emphasis on ideal physical types. Adolescents, and indeed adults, who look different from current ideals of physical attractiveness sometimes feel plain or out of place. The most important thing for any adolescent is to come to terms with their appearance, and to keep fit and healthy, rather than worry about how they think they should look.

Adolescents who are attractive to others often feel more confident and at ease. Sometimes it may appear as if they do not worry about their looks, yet they too may go through a phase where they suffer doubts about their appearance.

Some adolescents become anxious over particular aspects of their physical development. Girls sometimes worry that their breasts may be either too big or too small; boys may be anxious about the

size of their penis. Both sexes worry about the spots that hormone changes sometimes cause. But as adolescents become more accustomed to their new bodies, these worries tend to diminish. Before this happens, adolescents sometimes need extra time alone when they can think about themselves and some of their worries in peace. This need for privacy is quite natural, although often misunderstood and not respected by parents and brothers and sisters.

Adolescents need time alone to get used to the changes that are taking place in their bodies.

SEXUAL DEVELOPMENT

THE RELEASE of hormones into the body during puberty is the signal for both boys and girls to start their sexual development.

Both boys and girls experience strong sexual feelings during adolescence.

Sexual development sometimes gets under way as early as nine or ten years old; occasionally it starts late on in the teens. But for most adolescents sexual changes happen between the ages of eleven and thirteen, with girls usually starting at a younger age than boys.

GiRLS' SexuaL DeveLOPMeNT

The first clear sign in girls of the changes to come is the appearance of the breast bud. This is just a small bump at first. At the same time as this is happening, a girl's external sexual organs become more rounded, and her internal sexual organs develop. Eventually her ovaries will begin to release the eggs that have been stored there since birth, and she will begin to have periods (menstruation).

The process of menstruation, from the release of the egg (ovulation) to the beginning of a period.

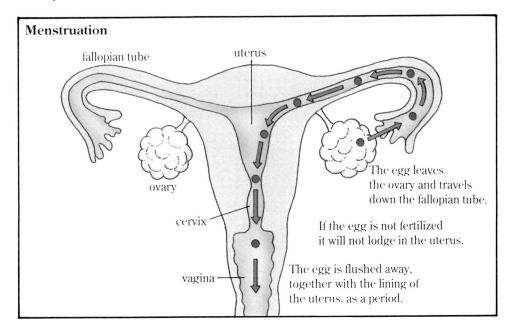

Menstruation

fallopian tube

uterus

ovary

cervix

vagina

The egg leaves the ovary and travels down the fallopian tube.

If the egg is not fertilized it will not lodge in the uterus.

The egg is flushed away, together with the lining of the uterus, as a period.

This girl is going through a ceremony of purification following her first period.

A period occurs when an ovum (egg) leaves one of the two ovaries and travels down a thin tube to the uterus. While the ovum is still in one of these 'fallopian tubes', it can become fertilized by a male sperm if a couple have sexual intercourse. If fertilized, the ovum then becomes attached to the lining of the uterus and starts growing into an embryo. But if the egg arrives in the uterus unfertilized, it passes unnoticed out of the body. Some of the uterus lining, which has temporarily thickened up in readiness for the attachment of a fertilized egg, then breaks down and is rejected too. The lining trickles out of the vagina over the following few days in the form of a few tablespoonsful of blood. This process is repeated once roughly every twenty-eight days, although there may be several months' gap between a girl's first few periods.

Girls who start menstruating early sometimes get teased by their peers. Later, however, their increased physical maturity may give them more prestige among their age group.

Some girls experience a certain amount of premenstrual tension (PMT). Building up just before menstruation, this can include headaches, mild depression, tearfulness, weight-gain or tiredness. Some girls suffer quite severe pain during menstruation, such as bad backaches or abdominal cramps. Both PMT and period pain may respond to medication and exercise.

BOYS' SEXUAL DEVELOPMENT

The release of hormones in boys during puberty leads to an increase in size of the testes and penis. The testes begin to produce sperm during puberty. Sperm are tadpole-like cells carried in a fluid called semen. During sexual intercourse, this fluid is ejaculated from the penis. If the sperm then meet a female's ovum, fertilization may take place.

Boys begin to experience more frequent erections at this time. These are often triggered by sexual feelings, but may happen at other times too. For example, at night boys may have an erection and ejaculate sperm.

sexual feelings

Sexual feelings during adolescence vary greatly. Some adolescents may experience a crush on someone unobtainable, like a teacher or pop star. This may be someone of the same sex.

Having a crush on someone and fantasizing about what it would be like to be with them may be a way of trying out sexual feelings without the problems of being seriously involved. Masturbation is another way in which adolescents find out about sex and their bodies.

Many adolescents experience a period of sexual attraction to the same sex. For some people this will be a passing phase, leading to heterosexual

Girls waving and screaming at a pop concert. Having a crush on a pop hero is a way of trying out sexual feelings without getting involved.

Homosexuality is often regarded with suspicion and prejudice. Adolescents who think they may be homosexual may find it difficult to talk about their feelings because of this.

relationships, but other adolescents know early on in life that they are mainly homosexual.

For adolescents who do have strong sexual feelings for people of the same sex, it can be difficult to discuss these feelings openly. In many societies, homosexuality is still not talked about, and homosexual relationships are not recognized or are illegal. In most countries, books, newspapers and television programmes give a negative impression of homosexuals. Even in those societies where heterosexual relationships are discussed more openly, parents and teachers may feel uneasy about discussing homosexuality with young people. They may feel that they are somehow 'encouraging' adolescents to become homosexual, particularly if homosexual relationships between young people are against the law.

However, when adolescents try to bottle up homosexual feelings, they often become depressed and isolated. Their work may suffer, they may lose self-confidence and feel unable to mix with other people. If a young person is worried about homosexual feelings, it is important that they find someone with whom they can discuss their fears. Gay youth groups help adolescents meet, so that they can talk to other people who have similar feelings and experiences. Fears about homosexuality can also be reduced by getting to know older men and women who feel happy and comfortable about being homosexual.

sexual behaviour

Early sexual relationships often involve no more than kissing, hugging and holding hands. The age at which people start to have sexual intercourse varies enormously. It is influenced by social customs, friends' experiences, and opportunity, as well as personal choice. The media also play a significant role in the development of attitudes towards sex. Advertisements, films, newspapers and pop music, for example, tend to glamorize sex and link it with material wealth.

Most countries have laws stating the minimum age for sexual intercourse; this is known as the age of consent. It is difficult to know at what age people start to have sexual intercourse, as it is not something that people are necessarily truthful about. Because more boys than girls may see sex as something to boast about, they may claim to have had sexual intercourse when they have not. However, a North American study found that in 1979 48.5 per cent of seventeen-year-old girls and 55.7 per cent of seventeen-year-old boys claimed to be sexually experienced.

Attitudes towards sex among people in the developed world have changed greatly over the past forty years. For example, sex outside marriage has become much more acceptable in some cultures. Once adolescents do become sexually active, unwanted pregnancy and sexually transmitted diseases become an important consideration for both boys and girls. Sex education is important in helping to reduce the incidence of these.

The people who support sex education claim that it helps prevent teenage pregnancy. Low pregnancy and abortion rates among adolescents are associated with the availability of free or low-cost family planning services, and timely information about sexuality and contraception in schools or the media.

Adolescents who have unprotected sex are at risk of catching sexually transmitted diseases, including AIDS. Although all the ways the AIDS virus (HIV) can be transmitted are not yet known, wearing a condom does reduce the risk of infection for both homosexuals and heterosexuals.

M€NT∂L GROWTH

Adolescents are able to tackle more complex school work as they develop mentally.

ADOLESCENCE IS a time of rapid mental development. Childish reasoning is gradually abandoned as adolescents begin to think in more adult ways. To understand how this happens it is necessary to look for a moment at the type of reasoning common when children are younger.

"Give me a place to stand and I will move the Earth"
Archimedes, 300BC

THe GROWTH OF THOUGHT

Young children find it easier to understand actual situations, objects and events, rather than imaginary ones. Science, for example, will therefore make more sense to them when they can see the materials upon which a lesson is based. In a history lesson, a child will understand more about a castle or fort if they can either visit one or refer to a picture.

Adolescents gradually develop the ability to think about ideas. When asked, for example, to discuss voting, an adolescent will not simply talk about putting a completed ballot paper into a box, but will be able to think about the fuller implications of voting, for example in a secret ballot, and what exactly this implies for a political system such as democracy. When asked to comment on societies where voting is illegal, adolescents should be able to imagine a

Young women demonstrating in London. Adolescents often hold strong views on issues that affect them.

situation like this and then assess it. This type of thinking, known as abstract thought, occurs after adolescents have developed the wider vocabulary necessary for this complex reasoning.

LOGIC AND IMAGINATION

Adolescents also become better at the step-by-step type of reasoning known as logical thought. This is something that is often beyond younger children. Take the situation of two toy cars racing each other. A young child will say that the one passing the finishing line first is the fastest, even though this car may also have been given a massive start over the other one. But adolescents will take this advantage into consideration when asked to make their judgement.

In this way an adolescent is able to take many more factors into account when reasoning. This ability to suspend immediate reactions and make more considered judgements is usually well beyond the capacity of younger children.

Using logic allows adolescents to think more efficiently in other ways. They may now be capable of noting that society does not always practise what it preaches. Such awareness of the differences that often exist between what people claim to believe and what they actually do sometimes leads adolescents to condemn society as hypocritical.

These changes in thinking mean that many adolescents become argumentative, sometimes feeling so convinced that they are right that they become impatient with any opposition. Experience of

changing their own minds, and seeing others change theirs, will eventually persuade most of them that no one is right about everything.

LANGUAGE SKILLS

Improved skills in language during this period mean that adolescents get more from what they are reading. Younger children often misunderstand what they read. But when a writer chooses to be sarcastic, for example, by saying one thing but really meaning another, the adolescent is now better able to understand what is being implied.

Adolescents are able to apply new mental skills to their reading.

In many countries, more and more time is taken up by school work as adolescents prepare for important examinations.

Adolescents are also better at recognizing the meaning of proverbs and other figures of speech. They are usually more skilled in seeing the jokes contained in adult cartoons or stories. Looking beyond immediate appearances for hidden meanings is an extremely useful ability that only starts developing effectively during this period.

Young children often find writing very hard, labouring for long periods over a simple 'thank you' letter and writing shapeless stories where everything runs together. Some of the problem here is lack of agility in handwriting, but young children also find it hard to organize ideas clearly. The result is often a muddled story in which it is difficult to distinguish the main events.

Growing intellectual power enables adolescents to learn how to plan and organize their thoughts, and to recognize the needs of the reader. For example, when writing essays at school they will learn to start with a general introduction, and at

the essay's conclusion try to draw every strand of the argument together.

In conversation adolescents also become more skilful at conveying opinions, and pause more often to listen to what others have to say. The stories they tell often have more point than before, and their jokes may now be much better than the painful efforts they once used to try out on long-suffering friends and relations.

When talking to others, instead of addressing everyone in the same way, adolescents are now aware that parents, teachers or visitors may each expect to be talked to in a slightly different manner. So when adolescents are talking to someone who comes from a different background, they are now better at making allowances for what the other person may or may not already know. Unlike younger children, they will no longer assume that everyone else possesses exactly the same range of beliefs and knowledge as they do themselves.

Discovering how to communicate with other people is as important as learning facts and figures.

PSYCHOLOGICAL DEVELOPMENT

Many adolescents believe that other people are forever judging them. When walking along a corridor or diving into a swimming pool, for example, they may feel convinced that everyone within range is closely inspecting everything they are doing, down to the last tiny detail. Some adolescents play to an imaginary audience even when on their own. This is a form of egocentrism, which is common in children and adults; a painful self-consciousness that makes adolescents particularly sensitive to even mild criticism.

When making judgements about others, adolescents may now assess friends by taking into account what they may have been like in the past, as well as how they may be behaving at the moment. Sometimes adolescents may decide that a friend is being driven by feelings hidden from those who know them less well. All this marks the move away from childlike instant judgements to thinking about others in deeper, more perceptive ways. This greater ability to understand others often leads adolescents to chat for long periods about people they know. Comparing their thoughts on somebody with those of other people helps develop a more rounded impression of others' personalities.

Adolescents often develop firm opinions about the nature of their own selves. Sometimes they will spend hours thinking about what they most like or dislike about their own personality, or how exactly they should behave when faced with different social situations. Occasionally they will conclude that they

are the only ones ever to have had the thoughts or feelings they are experiencing. This is almost always untrue, but they will often continue to believe this until they have enough self-confidence to share such private thoughts with friends. When this happens, they generally discover that others have had almost the same hopes, fears and worries as they have themselves.

Occasionally this new process of looking into the self can lead adolescents to strong self-criticism, first identifying and then condemning every tiny fault they think they possess. These critical powers may be directed at parents and teachers too.

Adolescents can be easily hurt by even mild criticism of their looks or behaviour.

FaMiLY ReLaTiONSHiPS

FAMILY RELATIONSHIPS tend to change when children reach adolescence. As the adolescent member of the family establishes a more adult personality, the rest of the family have to adjust.

Changes in family relationships can cause adolescents to feel insecure. Discussing worries with a close friend may help them to adjust.

This is difficult not only for the adolescent, but also for their parents and brothers and sisters. Often a whole new set of rules has to be established. These changes are not necessarily bad; adolescent development can improve family relationships with time.

As children become more mature, their relationship with their parents often improves.

iNDePeNDeNCe

Adolescence is said to be a period of increasing independence. However, some adolescents may find that they want more freedom than their parents allow, and this can lead to problems at home. Even though their parents may be spending less time with them than before, adolescents may still feel rather too much under parental control.

Some parents do not really want their children to become more independent. Such parents, often brought up strictly when they were young, may be unable to understand that, as times have changed, so

Conflicts may arise when adolescents are forced to conform to their parents' wishes.

have ideas about child-rearing. If these parents try to enforce rigid standards on adolescents who do not see the point of them, it can create friction.

Other parents are eager to relinquish their authority and control, allowing their adolescents to do whatever they like. This can result in confusion and a feeling of being unwanted and uncared for; adolescents need guidance and support in their lives, as well as a certain amount of independence.

CONFLICTS WITH PARENTS

As adolescents start to question things and to develop their own ideas, family arguments often become more common. When they were younger most would have been inclined to accept what a parent said without particularly thinking about it. But now they often require good reasons from their parents as to why they should do something, and if these reasons are unconvincing they may refuse to do what is asked. Parents may feel exasperated at this sudden loss of control over their children's behaviour, and may react by being even stricter, in an attempt to re-establish their authority.

This period of development is a time when people generally experiment with different styles of appearance, as well as various types of music, political opinions and so on. Many arguments during adolescence centre on appearance, for example, dress and haircut. Parents often feel that if their children are 'unsuitably' dressed, then this shows poor upbringing and therefore reflects upon them. Adolescents, on the other hand, feel they should take responsibility for the way they look.

Adolescents are often harshly critical of their parents. This is because they are now better able to compare their parents with what they think a parent should be. Younger children are usually content to accept their mother and father unquestioningly but adolescents may want something impossibly ideal.

A further reason for parent–adolescent conflict has more to do with parents' lives: the parents' relationship may be going through a difficult patch, or there may be money problems. Adolescents, with their large appetites and expensive tastes, often cost parents much more than before, sometimes putting a strain on family finances. When adolescents consider their future careers, this occasionally prompts a parent to start wondering what they themselves have achieved in life. If they come to the conclusion that their own future prospects now look rather dull in comparison with what their children might go on to do, this can be a further source of unhappiness and tension for parents.

Adolescents also sometimes make their parents feel particularly self-conscious about their own progress towards middle or old age. As their

Going to parties and dressing in the latest fashions is part of the fun of being an adolescent.

children grow in strength and sexual attractiveness, parents sometimes start waking up to the fact that they themselves are no longer young or particularly good-looking. Sometimes this realization leads to quite immature behaviour on the part of parents, anxious to prove that they too can still attract the opposite sex.

The conflict between adolescents and parents seems to peak during the mid-teenage years. In most families the arguments that take place can often be no bad thing. At best they provide adolescents with a good debating ground within which to develop their own ideas and attitudes, sometimes in line with what their parents believe, sometimes not.

Parents who refuse to get involved in conflicts may never give their children the chance to discover

Parents may feel dissatisfied with their own lifestyles and envious of the opportunities their children have.

through argument exactly what they think. Argument-free households may be quieter places, but not necessarily healthier ones.

Despite the arguments, most adolescents maintain close relationships with their parents. While there may be some strong disagreements at home, most adolescents are still more influenced by their parents than they are by anyone else over major decisions to do with education or choice of job. If an adolescent has fallen out with friends, it is still very often a parent to whom they turn for advice on what has gone wrong and how best to put it right.

Loving relationships with parents are just as important in adolescence as they are in childhood. Knowing that they are still valued at home provides young people with important stability during an otherwise often rather uncertain time. A sense of security also helps establish the self-confidence necessary to make firm relationships with friends of their own age.

Adolescents lacking support at home often suffer as a result. Sometimes they may behave in an attention-seeking way, as if trying to demand that someone should take notice of them. Their own self-image may be badly damaged if they feel that their parents no longer value them.

SIBLINGS

Younger brothers and sisters sometimes resent the way in which adolescents withdraw, spending more time alone. They may react by invading the adolescent's privacy because they want to re-establish the closeness that existed before. If adolescents have never got on well with their younger siblings, then quarrels may arise due to personality clashes that have always existed.

Some adolescents take a close interest in their younger brothers and sisters. These siblings may in return hero-worship them, trying to copy what they do and say. Youngsters can sometimes communicate with adolescent siblings more easily than with their parents, especially over matters such as dealing with friends, coping at school, physical appearance and sexual knowledge. In this way adolescents can be valuable teachers for their younger siblings, passing on useful information.

As adolescents grow older, they may feel more caring and protective towards younger brothers and sisters.

During a divorce, adolescents need just as much comfort and support as younger children. Choosing which parent to live with can be particularly painful.

DIVORCE

Divorce is usually an upsetting experience for children at any age. Adolescents may be better at coping with it if they have friends they can confide in. But if parents lean on their children for emotional support, adolescents may find themselves getting drawn into the divorce to an uncomfortable extent. They may also feel partly responsible for whichever divorced parent they are now living with. Divorce can be made less harrowing if adolescents can keep in close touch with both parents and if they are reassured that they do not need to take sides.

If parents remarry, then problems may arise with stepparents, as new relationships have to be established. Adolescents may feel very protective towards their own parent, and find it difficult to accept a new person sharing their family life.

FR*i*eNDS, SCH*oo*L *a*ND Le*i*su*R*e

ADOLESCENCE IS a time for developing relationships with friends, teachers and other adults. Social contacts of this sort outside the family can help an adolescent develop new ways of thinking and behaving. Through these friendships adolescents are gradually able to build up a life outside the family.

Shared political beliefs have brought this group of young people together.

FRiENDS

In dress, language, ideas and general behaviour, adolescents are often influenced by friends and acquaintances. The desire to belong to a group of like-minded friends can be very strong. Once accepted by a group, adolescents can check more easily on what others of their age are doing, in order to make comparisons with their own tastes and habits. They may try out different kinds of behaviour, occasionally doing things that bewilder their parents, as they seem to be out of character. However, learning when to resist group influence is just as important an aspect of social development as is making friends.

The type of group adolescents join may be determined by their interests; for example, if they are athletic, they might be attracted to a group where the shared interest is sport. A further determining factor in choice of group may be status. A person of average ability in school may feel their confidence boosted by joining a group of adolescents who are less successful at school work.

Not all adolescents become members of groups. Those whose strong individual interests take up most of their time often prefer to stay on their own. There are also adolescents who want to join a group but who lack the confidence to do so. These may go around together, not always because they enjoy each other's company but because they feel no one else will have them. These adolescents often have a low opinion of themselves, whatever their outward show of confidence.

BOYFR*ie*NDS *a*ND G*i*RLFR*ie*NDS

During early adolescence, people tend to spend the majority of their leisure time with the same sex. Gradually, however, most adolescents become interested in the opposite sex and start going out with them. Most people feel nervous about this to begin with because it involves learning a whole new set of social skills. Although they will be able to use the friendship skills they have already built up, the majority of adolescents will not know how to behave in sexual situations.

Adolescent knowledge about sexual behaviour usually comes from friends. Although there is a rapid increase in sexual drive during adolescence, many people's early sexual experiences are also a result of curiosity or peer pressure.

Not all adolescents go out on dates. Some may not be interested yet; others may lack self-confidence. Some may enjoy spending time with the opposite sex but not want to get physically involved.

Adolescents may enjoy going out together but deciding whether to have sex can put a strain on the relationship.

SCHOOL

In most parts of the world, people spend the majority of their days during adolescence in school. School is therefore an important area of influence, not just from the point of view of lessons but because of the relationships that are built between pupils, and between pupils and teachers. Pupils are generally happiest at schools that treat them like independent young adults rather than like children. But they also need strong support in the form of advice, well-organized teaching and after-school activities.

Ideally a school should combine a caring interest in pupils with a well-structured, stimulating environment. However, the reality of school can be quite different. Some adolescents feel that what they are learning at school is of little relevance to their lives or futures. Many schools still value brain power above other skills. This can make pupils who prefer practical work, for example, feel as if their abilities are not worthwhile. Those who view school as a training ground for work may feel they are wasting their time there if unemployment is so high that they are unlikely to get a job anyway. Truancy and disruptive behaviour are often the result of such feelings.

Teachers have an important bearing on how adolescents feel about themselves. Pupils who are labelled as problems tend to see themselves that way. Teachers' attitudes can therefore have an influence on the happiness and motivation of their pupils.

Leisure

Many schools provide opportunities for organized leisure activities. These include sports and club-type activities such as drama. However, the majority of adolescents spend a great deal of their leisure time talking or being with people the same age in youth clubs (if these are available), in each other's homes or in the street.

Although some adults may think that adolescents are not doing anything constructive when they stand around talking, this is actually an important element in the development of friendship and communication skills.

Teachers play an important part in building up their pupils' self-confidence.

*i*DEN*t*iTY

Religious beliefs form part of a person's sense of identity.

IN THE period between leaving childhood and becoming an adult, adolescents often think about what sort of person they would like to be. They may also find themselves wondering who exactly they are at the moment. This leads to experimenting with different ideas, attitudes and types of behaviour, in a way that is sometimes bewildering for adults. This is, however a natural part of growing up.

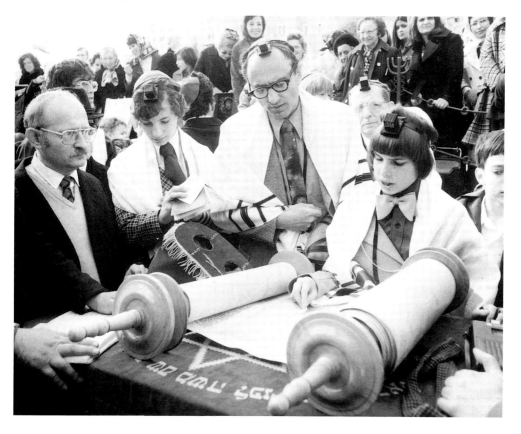

Identity is something that is built up gradually throughout life. It is made up of an individual's personal history – such as their culture, country, family and religion – as well as their personality, ambitions, attitudes and so on. Adolescence is an important time for building identity because it is a time when people begin to make their own choices and decisions, and to experiment with different roles.

Whereas young children often merely imitate their parents in ideas and attitudes, adolescents have to make more of their own choices about what to believe or how to behave. Adolescents' ideas about politics, religion, fashion, music and many other topics often change rapidly, as they attempt to find out what they really believe.

This uncertainty about what they think can be confusing for adolescents, and occasionally leads to what has been called an identity crisis. This

Rebels against society? Experimenting with different fashions helps adolescents to decide what sort of people they really are.

describes the state of mind when someone feels so confused that they may doubt whether they possess any fixed beliefs, ambitions or desires at all. Identity crises can happen at any time in life but the peak time for such identity confusion occurs between the ages of fifteen and eighteen. After that time people usually have a firmer idea about themselves and what they want out of life.

Parents often forget what they were like as adolescents and feel bewildered by this stage of development. They can help by listening to their children, rather than lecturing them, and by being patient while this state of confusion is gradually worked out.

THE FUTURE

Deciding what to do in the future – deciding on type of work or further study, for example – is part of building an identity. Some adolescents put off the moment when they have to think about their future.

Developing special interests can help people to decide what to do after leaving school.

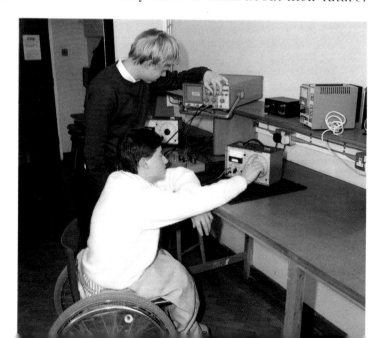

Faced by difficult decisions, they avoid them, concentrating instead on day-to-day activities. Others make a firm commitment to a certain ambition early on. These adolescents are often very single-minded. Some others are dominated by their parents' ideas of what they should do, and do not question this until much later in life.

CLOSE RELATIONSHIPS

The ability to establish a warm, close relationship with someone else also helps in establishing a sense of identity. This can prove difficult for adolescents who remain uncertain of themselves and are still unsure about what they are looking for in themselves, let alone in anyone else.

Adolescents can also be so taken up with their own feelings that they are often unaware of what other

A boy helping out on his father's farm. Some adolescents feel pressurized into joining the family business when they leave school.

49

people are like. Sometimes they fall in love with what they want someone else to be, rather than what that person really is.

People vary in their ability to maintain close friendships. Those who already possess a strong sense of identity will often have few difficulties. But many adolescents find it difficult to be themselves when they approach others. Instead, they try to behave in a way that they think the other person will admire or find attractive. A naturally gentle boy trying to act tough, for example, will end up feeling that no one likes him as he really is. Those who lack self-confidence sometimes start on a relationship, only to back out once they feel they can no longer handle it or keep up the pretence. These individuals often have to wait until they are older and more self-assured before they can trust themselves and others enough to form a stable, long-term relationship.

Some people prefer to spend time with just one or two close friends; others enjoy being part of a group.

MORAL DEVELOPMENT

Another important stage in the growth of a sense of identity comes when individuals develop their own ideas about what is right or wrong. Faced by difficult moral questions, young children tend to repeat what their parents or other adults would say. But because of the adolescent's developing powers of thought, many are now better able to think for themselves. They may now find themselves taking a very different view from their parents on issues such as sexual morality or politics, for example. In doing so, they are taking one further step along the path to establishing themselves as independent, individual beings.

While younger children answer a question like, 'Is it wrong to steal?' with a simple, 'Yes', adolescents may often reply more on the lines of, 'It all depends'. If the person stole to save a life, for example, the adolescent might then say that in some circumstances stealing could be justified. Other moral questions that appeared straightforward to the adolescent when they were younger may seem more complex now. They may therefore think more carefully before making judgements.

In discussion during lessons at school, adolescents should be provided with the opportunity to learn to think for themselves and to listen to others. If they come across an interesting new opinion, they sometimes absorb it into their own ideas. Other pupils, as well as teachers, can help this learning process by contributing different ideas.

PROBLEMS DURING ADOLESCENCE

ADOLESCENCE IS often described as a problem time. This is unfair and inaccurate in the majority of cases. Young children and adults can also have severe problems, while many people have a trouble-free adolescence.

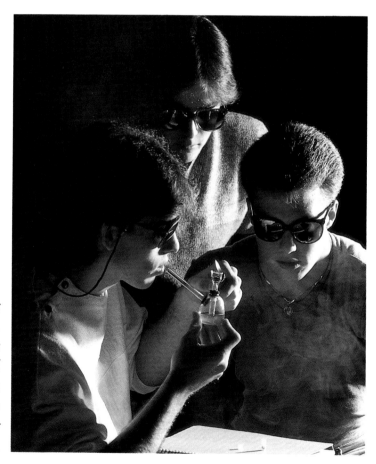

Teenagers smoking crack. Such drugs are expensive and many people have to steal to support their drug habit.

Because adolescence is a time of experimentation, there are certain problems that may arise, although these can develop at other times of life too. This chapter deals with some of the problems that adolescents may experience.

DRUG abuse

Adolescents may experiment with physically non-addictive soft drugs, such as cannabis. Some may go on to try more dangerous drugs, like heroin, cocaine and crack.

A person's reasons for trying drugs are often linked to the desire to be like everyone else in a group, to appear adult and 'cool'. Adolescent males are particularly likely to be influenced by this sort of pressure. Soft drugs may supply a feeling of well-being over a short period. But those who consume them in large quantities often end up by becoming distanced from others, and unable to concentrate, either in lessons or anywhere else. For this reason school work generally suffers and social life becomes limited to those with the same drug habits.

The majority of adolescents take drugs only as a passing experimental phase. Those adolescents who become regular consumers of drugs may, for example, have parents with drug habits themselves. Even if they do not use the same drugs, their parents may be dependent on alcohol or tobacco. Some drug-using adolescents may be imitating what their best friends are doing. These friends are often older than they are, suggesting that the adolescents concerned may be having difficulty in relating to people of their own age. Drugs are also seen as an escape from boredom, depression or problems at home. Adolescents sometimes use drugs to relax in an attempt to overcome awkwardness or shyness in company. The relief offered by drugs does not last long.

ALCOHOL

Both alcohol and tobacco are drugs. The reasons for taking them are generally the same as for other drug use. In other words, they may help relaxation, make the user feel adult and so on. The difference between alcohol and other drugs is that many parents drink alcohol, advertisers promote it, and it is therefore more socially acceptable. The age at which young people are legally allowed to buy alcohol is, in fact, often seen as the age at which they become officially adult.

Almost every adolescent tries alcohol at some stage. Some will also drink to excess on occasions. To start with, drinking alcohol is often part of the normal adolescent urge to experiment with something new. But with some adolescents the end results are very serious, particularly for those who turn to alcohol regularly in order to reduce anxiety or tension. While many adolescents may find themselves doing this on a few occasions, some eventually rely on alcohol as support for almost everything they do. Such adolescents often come from heavy-drinking families where there may also be tension and unhappiness.

SMOKING

Tobacco is a drug that has also been socially acceptable. This is less true now and it is banned in many public places, particularly in the USA.

Despite the known health risks – which include numerous forms of cancer; bronchitis; emphysema; infertility; hardening and narrowing of the arteries which can lead to heart attack, stroke, gangrene or angina – some adolescents still take up smoking. Heavy advertising by the tobacco industry encourages people to see smoking as something fashionable and socially desirable.

The majority of adults who smoke regularly started in childhood or adolescence. Very few people take up smoking after the age of twenty. Although adolescents may not think they are addicted if they are smoking only one or two cigarettes a week, by the time a person has had four cigarettes they stand a 90 per cent chance of becoming a regular smoker.

Once smoking was part of the image. Now fewer people see cigarettes as a fashion accessory.

Young adolescents playing with fire in Liverpool.

When tobacco advertising is reduced and smoking is discouraged in public places, adolescents (like everyone else) tend to smoke less. Many schools now teach the dangers of smoking. In group discussions afterwards, adolescents can help each other to decide to stop smoking.

JUVENILE DELINQUENCY

Juvenile delinquency is a term used to cover various types of criminal behaviour by young people, for example vandalism, theft, and drug-taking. While the majority of adolescents are law-abiding, some regularly break the law. There are a number of possible reasons for this, such as personality problems, difficulties at home, living in an area where there is little provision for young people, and so on. For some it might be a dramatic way of demonstrating their independence. Others might turn to criminal behaviour when they feel they have no chance of success in life. Delinquent behaviour is often an expression of dissatisfaction with society.

Strong group pressure, recognisable in gangs of youths, can also encourage delinquency, particularly in areas where there is already a high crime rate and where there are few provisions for young people. Serious crime committed by adolescents can have disastrous effects on their lives. The punishment that follows occasionally disrupts their education so seriously that hopes of a good job or further training disappear. Committing serious crime also puts adolescents at odds with the rest of society, including people of their own age.

In order to build their identity and to feel as if they belong, adolescents need to belong to groups and take part in group activities. It may be that delinquent activities provide the same things that any other group activity provides, for example relief from boredom and a feeling of belonging and friendship.

Depression and suicide

Depression is something that often happens during adolescence. This may sometimes be caused by the hormonal changes that occur during the rapid physical development of adolescence. There is also the possibility that a tendency for severe depression can be inherited.

Most adolescents experience a certain amount of depression at times, and while this is always unpleasant , it is not usually something to worry about. Depression may be caused by the quite

People who threaten suicide are not always bluffing. They may be suffering from depression and need expert help.

normal periods of uncertainty and lack of confidence common to all adolescents. For example, some adolescents can become particularly upset about their physical appearance. Some go through a period of blaming themselves for various failures at school, work or in their social lives, even though this may not really be their fault.

In a very few cases, depression can lead to suicide attempts or even suicide itself. Suicide attempts have increased during the last forty years, particularly among adolescent males. People who attempt suicide often suffer from depression linked to long-term family difficulties. For such adolescents, a further personal set-back in life, coming on top of an already difficult situation, may occasionally act as the final blow.

PROBLEMS AT SCHOOL

Poor achievement at school can become a real problem during adolescence. Some pupils lack motivation, or else do not have the confidence to do well at school. They may then either withdraw from school through truancy, or try to disrupt lessons.

Other adolescents sometimes do badly at school because their parents have put too much pressure on them to succeed. If the adolescents resent this, they may occasionally express their anger by refusing to show an interest in school. Adolescents who are depressed for other reasons also often find it hard to work.

EATING PROBLEMS

Anorexia nervosa – a form of self-starvation – is a problem mainly affecting adolescent girls, though some boys suffer from it too. If starvation is kept up, anorexic adolescents may become dangerously thin, leaving themselves open to the risk of severe illness or death.

Curing anorexia nervosa is not easy; after a period of starvation people often find it hard to start eating again. Some experts think anorexia nervosa is caused by media obsession with being slim. Others see it as more to do with individual depression as a response to various family problems. Bulimia nervosa is another eating disorder that affects mainly women. Sufferers go on binges, eating enormous quantities of food, and then make themselves sick or take laxatives to prevent putting on weight. This is very dangerous and leads to hair-loss and vitamin deficiency, because the body is no longer given the chance to absorb what it needs from food. In severe cases it can lead to coma and even death.

HELP GROUPS

There are many special groups that help young people with the problems discussed above. Meeting other young people with the same problem can be a real help, especially in the case of alcoholics and drug users, whose social life may have revolved mainly around drink or drugs. Discovering that friendship from others does not necessarily have to involve heavy drinking or drug-taking is an important stage in ceasing to rely on these substances. For adolescents with eating disorders, specialist groups can provide them with the evidence that people will like them whether or not they are slim.

CONCLUSION

Despite the difficulties that can arise during the adolescent years, there is no evidence that adolescents suffer more problems than people of other ages. For some, life actually seems to get easier during this period. Going on to further education or starting a first job can be very enjoyable and exciting experiences, and many adolescents welcome the opportunity to make more decisions for themselves.

Young people are often given the impression that becoming an adult will resolve all the puzzles of adolescence. This is rarely the case. Many adults continue to face the crises of confidence they suffered in adolescence, but they are more experienced at dealing with these and therefore know they will recover. Adults tend to view adolescence as a period of freedom from responsibility and they sometimes tell teenagers that it is the best time of life. This is not necessarily true and can be worrying for adolescents who are having a bad time. Like any other period of life, adolescence for most people involves good times and bad times, and even the bad experiences and mistakes are a preparation for the future.

Adolescence can be an exciting time, as people form new relationships and enjoy new opportunities.

GLOSSARY

Abstract thought   Thinking about ideas, as opposed to actual people or objects.

Anorexia nervosa   An eating disorder that involves starvation to keep slim.

Anxiety   Intense worry or uneasiness.

Body image   The way someone feels about their appearance.

Bulimia nervosa   An eating disorder that involves periods of heavy eating, followed by deliberate vomiting or taking of laxatives to prevent putting on weight.

Conflicts   Struggles.

Depression   A feeling of extreme unhappiness.

Growth spurt   A sudden increase in height that signals the beginning of puberty.

Heterosexual   Someone who is sexually attracted to the opposite sex.

Homosexual   Someone who is sexually attracted to the same sex.

Hormones   Chemical substances in the body, responsible for the physical and sexual changes of puberty.

Identity   Who or what a person thinks he or she is.

Juvenile delinquent   A young criminal.

Logical thought   Step-by-step reasoning.

Menstruation   The monthly discharge of blood from the vagina that girls experience from puberty until the menopause.

Ova   The eggs produced by females that are capable of growing into a baby if fertilized by a male sperm.

Ovaries   Two organs in females that produce eggs.

Peers   People who are equal in age or rank.

Puberty   The time when children begin the physical and sexual development that leads to adulthood.

Self image   The way someone views themself.

Semen   The fluid in which sperm are carried.

Sibling   A brother or sister.

Sperm   A male cell, capable of fertilizing a female's egg.

Testes   The male organs in which sperm are produced.

Uterus   The womb.

BOOKS AND VIDEOS

BOOKS

Coleman, John *Family and Friends* (Wayland, 1990)
Coleman, John *Moods and Feelings* (Wayland, 1990)
Green, Christine *Body Changes* (Wayland, 1989)
Green, Christine *Growing Into Sex* (Wayland, 1989)
Meredith, Susan *Facts of Life: Growing Up* (Usborne, 1985)
Wellings, Kaye *First Love, First Sex: A Practical Guide to Relationships*
   (Thorsons, 1986)

VIDEOS

The following videos are available from Concord Video and Film
Council, 201 Felixstowe Road, Ipswich, Suffolk, 1P3 9BJ:

Danny's Big Night Looks at sex roles, sexual behaviour and peer
   pressure through studying the relationship of a young man and his
   girlfriend.
The Days of Fast and Abstinence The story of how a woman developed
   anorexia nervosa and some of the treatment she received.
Growing Up: Body, Feelings, Behaviour Designed for pre-adolescent
   children, this film looks at the physical, emotional and behavioural
   changes that occur during adolescence.
Kids' Stuff Solvent abuse and its consequences.
Parting Company How divorce is experienced by a couple and their two
   adolescent children.

PICTURE ACKNOWLEDGEMENTS

The publishers would like to thank the following for providing photographs: J. Allan
Cash 24, 37, 43; David Cumming *cover*; Orde Eliason/Link 20, 34, 36, 50; Greg Evans
Photo Library 29, 45; Eye Ubiquitous 41, 48; Format 21 (Pam Isherwood), 25, 33
(Jenny Matthews), 47 (Raissa Page); Sally & Richard Greenhill 39, 40; Robert Harding
Picture Library 10 (A. Morgan), 28 (David Hughes); John and Penny Hubley 27;
Hutchison Library 8, 13, 18; Impact Visuals 15 (Andrew Lichtenstein), 31 (Tony
Savino); Network 55, 56 (Mark Power); Samfoto 49; Shoot Photo Bank 4; Syndication
International 7; Tim Woodcock 32; ZEFA 16, 46, 52, 58, 61. The artwork is by Peter Bull.